Fairy Tales, Princesses, and Fables

You'll love spending hours of peace and calm bringing these artworks to life with color. Leave your worries behind, grab your favorite pencils and markers, and escape into a world of relaxation and the joy of creativity.

This book, is filled with inspiring designs of featuring all the classic characters of your childhood- Cinderella, Beauty and the Beast, Twelve Dancing Princesses, Snow White, Aladdin, Rapunzel, and so many more.

Fairy Tales, Princesses
&
Fables

this book belongs to:

_____
_____
_____
_____
_____

color test page

Made in the USA
Monee, IL
20 February 2022